T0161519

MENISCUS

ALSO BY SHANE NEILSON

Exterminate My Heart (2008, limited, private
    press edition)

Call Me Doctor (2006)

Alden Nowlan and Illness (2005, editor)

The Beaten-Down Elegies (2004, chapbook)

MENISCUS

SHANE NEILSON
MENISCUS

POEMS

BIBLIOASIS

FIRST EDITION

Library and Archives Canada Cataloguing in Publication

Neilson, Shane, 1975-
    Meniscus / Shane Neilson.

Poems.
ISBN 978-1-897231-60-9

    I. Title.

PS8577.E33735M45 2009   C811'.6   C2009-904585-0

 Canada Council **Conseil des Arts**
for the Arts **du Canada**

 Canadian   Patrimoine
Heritage   canadien

 ONTARIO ARTS COUNCIL
CONSEIL DES ARTS DE L'ONTARIO

We gratefully acknowledge the support of the Canada Council for the Arts, Canadian Heritage, and the Ontario Arts Council for our publishing program.

PRINTED AND BOUND IN CANADA

Spare those who know not what they do.

CONTENTS

Seized

Love Life

. . . bereft
Of anyone to please, it withers so,
Having no heart to put aside the theft

And turn again to what it started as,
A joyous shot at how things ought to be,
Long fallen wide. You can see how it was . . .

—Philip Larkin, "Home is So Sad"

Recovery

No poem in three years. The last one I wrote?
A suicide note.
Since then: three years without,

three years to bounce, to shun the pen
for a pageant of meds, for visits
to sessions, to take in credulous shrinks.

Poems shed less light the further I went.
Eventually, it was pitch, dark star, absent.
Yet words still sparked. I suppressed

them or let them fizz out. Once, they made me tick,
but I rejected them like a meal that made me sick.
Until today. Until, compressed,

a few words beckoned and those words, buoyant,
rose. I surveyed three barren years
and saw a poem, flaring there.

The Beaten-Down Elegies

My Father's Hands

Claim a plot of land your prison: boundaries
far as the cricks that keep a neighbour's farm
from creeping. The stern command to grow:
plough and harrow, till and sow, months of hoe-

blister turned callous. Then, time to reap
and sell, winter's cold repelled by summer
skin toughened until abuse is kin.
My prison wasn't the seasons, nor

was it acreage. It came in a pleated
hide that resisted nail-pricks, absorbed
the force of hammers.
                                    My father's hands
grew large from work, thickened from crush and cut.

Each battered nuance pressed on my face
and chest. Blows registered like a title
deed. Going out to the pasture, I could feel
just where our property led. With time

I could picture his hands in my head.
He beat a lien in me—his legacy
of workday pride and defeat. He carried me
across, then turned back to serve his sentence.

Instead

Timber! That tip, that turn,
the spin, the fall and crawl,
the slurred call for a boy
to prop a spun world,
the tossed seas of a man
flooded with rum. Attempt
to stand, shoulder-hoist
to buoy the drunk up
to crash back again,
the whup of lungs
on rock, breaking ribs.
Up again to stagger,
sway-backed stumble
of a man who drank
to drown his dream: to stand
on land he owned
and need not crawl on.
Instead:
fields bare, sprouting bush
and bottles. A short walk
to the shed turns muddy
all-fours odyssey,
his head lolling on the way
to bed, hauled by a child
with the wish he were dead.

Beaten-Down Elegy

His slurred breath heavy,
a pant as blood flows
from my mouth, the sawdust
dreams of a kid thrown
from a rafter to land
in copper straw. The dread
of Dad, down the ladder
and looming, steel-toes
inches from a broken
boy. He's on me now, blows
of closed hands, cries smothered
in the closed bellows
of my chest. His curses
nothing next to his bawling.

I stand. The hay in the loft
won't stack itself. I climb.
Below, a man who's stolen
my sound, shoulders heaving:
noise of a boy who's stomped
a favourite toy. I cough red
and grab twine. The breath again,
and he's there, throwing bales,
the thump of wet hay on wet hay.

Best Property in Sheffield

I used to think all that work, that primp
and preen, a waste, and you a coward—
until I heard we lost thirty thousand that year.
Your mind stuck on that. How wise
is it to sit down to a meal with moneyed
townsfolk on an outmoded steamboat
to celebrate failure? Each shovelful
a failure and still you lightly shoveled
shit onto sun-browned spots, fertilized
the green. I imagine you stepping over
the arched road that night and watching that boat
steam by, the hired band covering George Jones
and Loretta Lynn, taking some satisfaction
in the refusal of the tree shade on the bank,
thinned out thirty years ago, and not having to smile.

No Ring

Trajectories:
dishes leave the cupboards,
food on the wall,
refrigerator overturned,
TV kicked off its stand,
framed pictures punched,
furniture upended—
in the middle of this symphony,
my mother pulled off her wedding ring,
threw it as far as she could,
and, showing him the white line
on her finger, screamed
I'm not your wife anymore!

Then two successive snaps
and the sobbed admission
that the ring was in the yard.

I combed the grass for hours.
Night fell and no ring, no ring.
My parents returned from the hospital;
my mother gathered me
in her casted wrists
and tucked me in, whispering
that she had the ring
the whole time,
safely stowed.

Sunday Morning

Birch and balsam fir backed up
against the garage wall, stacked
to the rafters. The pile teeters
as more rows are built and crusted
snow on the sticks melts—
                              the cords
topple, my brother's engulfed
in a wave of wood. I jump
behind my father, his arms
outstretched, the flood hits us.

I wake to see him lifting
the mess his drunken crashing-
down craftsmanship has made,
excavating his kid
from the woozy fallen rows
his hands had laid.

Building a Bookshelf

His hands: grand rotting cathedrals,
buckskin inebriate brillos,

two huge cowcuffers.
Now they are demented,

they fly at buttons,
they skitter and slapdash,

they are shells, relics
of purpose. We put together

the bookshelf, plank
by plank, and those airplane

wings are undecided, fumble
with a nail, drop a hammer.

Tremors and the grip strength
of irony, parctic limbs. Each screw

excruciates, won't go in,
won't tighten. I take the driver

from him. He looks to me
to tell him next, and I tell him

what I never thought I would:
Let me handle it.

The Death of Uncle Jim

Hewn. Brittle-boned, at the end,
the wasting disease of age
sapped you, but still it could be said

you were chopped from wood,
a large knot for a mouth, old man's beard
for stubble, chips from a chipper

for eyes, and ears two broken stumps.
I met you best under cheeks reddened
from sap, on top of a tractor

that predated everyone but you,
straight effortless lines of a field
that predated everyone but you.

That field your measure,
the type of man everyone knew
by axe handles and calloused handshakes,

the last to stand of your predeceased,
of wood stoves with wide-open drafts
propped open by a matchbook.

A bachelor, with gleaming chips
and old-growth smell, I never knew
if you knew love, I never dared

ask, and I heard you died,
and what does one say to death?
You might say, *A job proper,*

and the last time I saw you
it was with your nephew, my father,
in the gazebo with piano and fiddle,

two truncal men, big trees bending
down, who never breathed
a word of it to work,

who breathed it then.

Flood, Sheffield 1973

It's biblical. Every year
it comes: Revelations
for a kid who rides his tires
and makes a trough, who watches

the ill-advised basement fill,
who hears the Emergency
Measures Organization
porkbarrelers trill their alarmist

klaxons and advise: *Get out.*
Men in red hats, knowing
that for the disastered,
this is their disaster.

We were born here
and we will all die here
and radio voices talk
of the bright side: how this

is life-gift to the flood plain.
Old men turn down the volume
and speak darkly of Mactaquac
Dam and a lever pulled

in bureaucratic heaven.
The buoys on the river
are submarines, bellwether
tethered, and the river

is unfurled on us, a roughhouser,
a renovator, and there may be
a death, the ninety-year-old
slipper-on-a-puddle, and here

it is a surprise what floats by,
and what floats. Look at the houses:
see the watermark of years
withstood. The water is always

a bet, a wherefore, and we are
already saved in the flooded
Presbyterian, we await
the water rent to blood,

we await a surprise: a big branch
goes by, this is Godot
in the Saint John River Valley.
A kid will bike by soon.

Roadside Vegetable Stand

Part of the weather, it sits. It looks
forgotten and reforgotten.

I have never seen it bear fruit,
have never seen a child man the stand,

selling cabbages or pumpkins.
I have seen it alone, under

a sun that bleaches it blander,
usurping the green, tattered canopy;

I have seen it out in the rain
being beaten into loneliness.

A farmer might have left it
for a moment, planning to return,

but fell in love with foreclosure.
The field offers us

this stand: a serious house
on serious earth it is,

an emporium of the farmer's first kiss
or his first inclination

to damn it all. For years
it has stood and has stood for

one good reason: our drive-by
appetites withstand care. The roadside

is one idea of order,
is fifteen years ago when the produce

was heavy and the farmer
did not abandon his worry

in the lee side of Route 2—instead,
he sold it to us.

Requiem on Old Route 2

He called out the names as we drove past the farms:
Moccasins, son sold the farm; Bridges, who died
after his wife died. And old Harvey
in the dilapidated clapboard, green eaves
heaving down, is 92, just out
of hospital. Then there were the bad Bagleys,
whose son ran away or died, the father
on an end-job somewhere in the tar sands,
and the Moffats, who closed the vegetable stand
a year ago. *Economics*, he said.

The names: deceased, dispersed, the road rerouted
seven years ago, the bloody river
iced over, old cement wharves cracked with age,
the only kind of farming here dairy
or cattle, the farmers buried
in the Baptist cemetery. All the kids I knew
gone, the men gone, the houses going, and my dad,
who gave nothing away, was naming his dead.

I was reading my dead: copies of Purdy
and Nowlan in the cab, and Mandelstam.
Poor John Clare and Kavanagh, who knew scenes
like this; Keats, because he studied medicine.
A snowstorm, our shiny truck bought
from the sale of the land. The icy wiper blades
were military drums. I drove slowly
past the drifting road. I had run out of names.

This is not a Rural Poem

The hills would roll if I say so. The stalks of corn that flank
      the road
are a million sentries, fields have been cultivated to lie fallow,
the barns are collapsible and don't know where to repair.
I am considering the sky, which is not a rural sky. It is full of
      city air
and clouds that slum, slumber, crawl, and roll despite my say
      so.
A man clambers to his mailbox, flag up; if it's not longhand,
it's junk. The oncoming cars are messengers by other means,
sent from lairs to land in other lairs, and all the criss-crossing
      sideroads
and concessions are magnificent dirt that dusts the underbelly
of concretized clouds. We have our say! The stone farmhouses
with vinyl additions are set apart, and we know why: out here
is one collective sigh. Men cannot get their sons to stay,
a nuisance tractor waits for cars to pass. Ruin the ruins:
shake the scene like a snow globe, shake some sense into the
      geriatric
habituals who, consulting almanacs, know their sky.
You will not disturb them. They plough snow from long
      laneways,
unlock their gates, are not pressed for time. Everyone drives
ten above the limit, it is the speed of life on the way,
there are miles and known miles the histories of hamlets,
a calendar day is crossed off, marked fair.

Love Poem

Love as colophon, the outgrowth
of disdain and anger's plenitude, the stronger
feelings that sharpen, then cleave
a thing to bits—this one, memory, another
resolve. No crude instrument is this.
Like blood and gasoline, the stains
come in increments, and a wish
is most precious of all. When pain
is purpose and the goal's achieved,
we can stagger arm-in-arm and look
back later, sated and relieved
that our parts were played. We took
our dooms and made them grievous;
granted in retrospect, wishes diminish.

Love in Practice

And love as blight or the kind of drought
that kills all green, leaving no work
but to weep and level the scorched stalks
with mortgaged machinery; the weather-beaten
crops that couldn't stand pestilence, frost
or love turned on itself. As soil erodes
and fronds arrest their growth, the season's lost
and fault is no one's. What's left are debts
that must be borne another year. I've tried
to touch that man who'd throttle a neck
as he did a cracked driveshaft, his grip belied
by how much he felt each failure, a black
and hardened ruin. Love as negative, in reverse,
but still in terms of violence: a kind of verse.

Rooted

No roots sown through rows were coughed
from the soil by ploughs; plants were grown
and sold at local stands. The crops
silent as I chose not to claim this place my own.
I was silent too, never saying so until I left,
the pleasure bursting forth: *I'm gone!*
That day follows me; I hear his laugh,
gross and lolling. *You'll be back, son.*
See you soon! Part of this nightmare's craft
is its grip on the bones, pulling memory
towards home. I ranged far from that
country fiefdom until the call of clemency
came. My mother on the phone: *He died.*
Can you come for the funeral? I did.

For my father

Is there a sorrow? If I look, it may be
creation. There are wisps of nothing,
an aurora of love that alights

on recall. Twinkling eye, hard fist: I do look.
I try to look like an accountant
at his ledger, but look instead on a fixed

post: totemic, obscure. In the end there is fear.
I try to see it the way an accountant
readies his red pen. It is a long time

since I strained to touch the sky; but still
I look back. The madness of choices
is witness; I remember

the blows, I remember the wishes.
I may have enough to look, I may crumple.
This is age, you may never know

the ambush, but this is not about you;
it is about being able to bear the load,
be it two cord of hardwood on a truck,

two cord in the ledger, the two cord of the heart,
two cord hauled out from backfields
and split with the hydraulic, carried in a child's arms

and piled head-high. It is difficult to count
how much, when, or why. I see a boy, a man;
I see grease stains and sawdust, and that salvation

spans countless fields, countless men, and it rests
where it is fair, where the fear is not
in neat rows, but in first-growth forests

that you will always be felling.

Manic Statement

Meniscus

A concave elegy, the liquid
hammock you sipped to drift
into oblivion; the bent
crevasse you crept into; the scythe
that dully cut your years
into depressions; a shallow ditch
for knowing better, a trench
for not caring; half a plump
teardrop; a drunk's undertow;
a half-eclipse; the cataract
of a chalice; a hollowed-out
hull that buckled with pouring,
the world skewed to your staggered
ellipse; and at last the thirsted
curve of lips that hallow.

Making Sense

I'm flummoxed: hock me up
in a hammock, spin me. All top-
heavy me, and let the lummox

go, watch the lunkhead
stagger, watch the ox
stomp, watch him at odd

angles, watch me. I'll tramp
and stamp, swagger dizzy and buzzed,
I'll be headlong, have no line, far-

flung, and as the world stems
to lacklustre, as I am stemmed,
as sense kilters, the hammock empty

and I've gone far, flung far
into a lesson: the world is not vested,
has no angle, it sets you, and atwitter

goes your head.

Christmas Morning

Joy persists amidst festive wreckage.
My girl laughs in an ornament jungle;
my wife takes pleasure from her innocent greed.
The tree is a last outpost's white flag.
Of if I could speak.

It is true, *I do dream:*
a cloud, field, and window;
the precipice of even ground,
My hand held by my beribboned girl.
I do dream.

Waking

If I bounce, I resolve,
there'll be no more waste or loss—
but that's all foolishness.

Blowing out
the candles, a big intake
and looking out a window but waking

to no difference. All the magic's of a pane;
I can see clouds I will never touch.
I am that fool.

Methods

To jump—
in this, real freedom.

No swallowing of gunmetal,
no deliberation of knots.

Only the urge of footsteps.
Then air.

Bird Men

No portals, and little
wisdom. Men jump from ledges,

hitting the sidewalk asleep
and dreaming of remote

perches. They grip metal
rungs and arch backs in practice,

perfecting pre-flight posture.
Trinkets fall from pockets,

cellphones trill on belts
tightened against this leathered

morning and handkerchiefs
billow in the wind. Drained

wallets strain against seat seams
and the cries of birds sound

softly. Men stretch arms
into albatross wingspans,

then hit earth with a thud.
Like crows that fly

from barren nests in search
of gallows to rest on

or cardinals that shed scarlet upon
the corpses of brethren, men balance

on railings and teeter.

It's Internal

The heart hiccoughs
blood, neurons are sluiced
in paralytic slush, meninges
aflame, limbs rigid, face
a spasm of smile. The time
it takes to stretch out
a finger. Yes, you. Mobile,
versatile, infernal. The soul
discharges its spent weight
and deflates, a flaccid
costume. Left, a man
with a routine—wake,
shower, shave, then work—
and tasks; overcast,
the only place, the only place,
where a deadhead tax
is extracted while the heart
thrashes, the brain seizes,
on again, on again.
How long before waking's
not enough, before
a sclerotic love becomes
a peephole through which
you can only see futile
horrors, perpetual
visitations, no cure?

Diagnosis

You've lived pain. Lived,
lived again. Been called

mad, addled, addicted.
You lived to injure—

just look at the linear
Braille on your wrists,

best-before corrugations
that contract with time,

become stiff upper lips.
What else do they augur?

Your fortune is to collide,
collapse and wake up

to wreckage. Sanity
is the worst injury, tomorrow

the wound.

Refrain

Just one day?
That's what

you say
until

tomorrow
and then

and then.
The game

of catch-up,
the price

of deferral,
the rosary

of "just one,"
lessons always

belated.
Ask instead:

Choke-chain love
too much

on your tongue?

Down

Think in terms of what you've lost:
You can't articulate pain,
but it's the one thing that's fast.

Bury you in verses; attend a mass
from the past with a gospel of lift,
the responsorial psalm:

save yourself, save yourself.
You knelt down on the plush bar.
The slow priest sang mass in pig-latin

as your mother prayed,
and your thoughts were not your own.
You knew the prayers by heart,

a pressing down, and you bore it
like the adulterous man with just one heart
after all: one to give,

one to cart.

Lithium

The missing element.
Goodbye to high,

a lift past low.
The places you'll go,

a straight line.
Almost a flatline.

Antidote? No.
Pyrrhic victory,

palliative,
salt of the earth.

Life on 8 Lane

I

Crackheads and messianics,
alcoholics, suicides. Those
who saw things, those
who heard voices—and one
woman afflicted with the constant
scent of butter. Crisp-capped
nurses, angels casting
the healing light of their halos.
Deuteronomy doctors, too,
their broad white sleeves
concealing magicks
to make you better. What
did you say? Why are they
writing this down? Which
doctor is best? What meds
are you on? Who can leave?
Who can we trust
to bring back the coffee?

II

Outside, people ducked
into shops, the city in perpetual
drizzle, and buses came late.
Red and black umbrellas
nudged elbows as they got
the IV in, as the bag began
to flow, as the aggrieved
wrestled orderlies, as he was pinned,
and the dark trees had a darker

halo, the sky a murderous
purple, as the patient dropped,
prone. Show over,
another paranoid asked
what are you looking at?
You pointed at raindrops
in golden sheen as headlights
doused their fall, as hurried
tires sloshed through puddles,
as people sat down
to the crib table again
and lunch was being served.

III

Life on a mental ward is just like life anywhere.
      —Alden Nowlan

A man could be talking to a wall
or me, he might speak of end times
or the food. A sick kid patrols the halls
with akathisia from his meds.
I learned that word in med school,
never guessing it had the slapping sound
of flip-flops.

         The sun still rises and sets,
gravity still grounds us, men need to talk,
hunger and love are eternal diversions.
The only difference is I might meet Jesus
or a woman convinced her spawn was the devil.

We all say hello in the halls,
good night at turn-in time
and I think of Nowlan's Bull Moose
between games of crib with my saviour.

There is no cure

Remember at five years old
there was an open field, beyond it rows of corn;
at twenty-five there is that same billowing field,
you are on it. The river threatens to rise this year;
it is pure. The doctors suggest salt; you tasted
it first out there, when the wind left it on your face.
The barn foundations cannot take another flood,
it could float away. At five you imagined
sitting on the tin roof, carried down the Saint John.
At twenty-five the doctors are in the field,
they ask you what you have to lose;
soon it will be time to mow and hay,
you tell them that the grass can only grow so high;
and what kind of loss would it have to be?
The doctors shake their heads like farmers do
when the season's bad. The river is for play
or for death; at five there was not enough day or choice;
at twenty-five you are on a perfect plain, unchanged;
the white coats on the plain do not talk of love,
though you do. This is when they shake their heads,
say you have a choice.

Bipolar

What it means: load
too much on one

side, then the other,
the equation

unbalanced, tipped,
toppled. All roads

are mad, we'd rather
another.

Feel the world's
tremors, heed them,

feel grace enough
to say, unaltered:

more.

Paranoia

A chalk outline is following me, it coughs like my department
      head.
A shivering chalk outline is following me; it needs a chalk
      overcoat.
A shuddering chalk outline is following me into the bedroom.
This chalk outline is lying in the bed, anticipating my
      missionary position.
A chalk outline is in the car, is in the office, is flying in the air
      like a bird, a plane,
like a chalk outline. A chalk outline is dancing like iPod
      commercials,
is doing the chalk cha-cha. There is an army of chalk outlines:
yellow chalk from teachers' blackboards, pink sidewalk chalk
      from a little girl's pail,
but the white chalk outlines are clearly in charge.
A chalk outline is following me. It is unflattering, because it is
      exact.
My chalk outline mimics the drinking of coffee.
A chalk outline is following me and is talking over me on a
      chalk cellphone.
The chalk outline says: *This guy is like nails on a blackboard.*
A chalk outline is following me, and it is very busy.
My chalk outline offers me advice: *chalk is cheap,*
you need to see the guy who traces bodies.
But my chalk outline is being followed by another chalk
      outline.

Seized

Open Head Injury

Out on the balcony our domestics raged
open air. Spectators gathered. Hatred's
throttled urge clenched my fists; I stalked
to the stairwell. Now memory blurs—

did you seize my arm, whisper
Don't go too low for me to hear?
I'm unsure. I felt a sensation
of push; off-balance, I crashed

through the railing. Two seconds
of free fall before my concrete splash,
blood compressed to high pitch
in the ears, din increasing

until I lay flat, flinching
in seizure's horizontals. My throat
gurgled and choked,
ballistic arms beat

to electrocuted songs, vision
a spattered easel of stars.
A grimace spread, tremors
built to furious swats.

Open head: wet,
I leaked from a hole. Above,
I saw a small, unrecoverable
beauty that overwhelmed

the waking world—
your face a small blot,
the sound of footsteps
rushing down stairs.

Postictal Period

Shocked faces approach
in bystander uprights

as I vibrate. The enemy
world struck *me* down—now

I'll strike back
with the rage of fists.

My slack mouth
and drowsy hate now bid

by agitated electric
dreams: rising, I regain

my feet and fight
arriving medics—

a sidewalk combat
that lurches, slurred.

Sound awash,
my cubist vision draws

strange outlines.
I collapse, wriggling

to an aftershock.
I'm seized, strapped

to a backboard, head locked
in a cervical collar.

Too violent, they tell you,
No passengers.

Seizure en Route

I

This discontented
body stretches
vertebrae to bend
and break—my neck
snaps back, the
seizure shotguns
and spreads. No mere
ripple in the head.
In one grand
discharge I
transmit all
that's been
touched and heard
in this life
of damage.

II

I felt your good riddance
in the fall. The rest is ambulance.
My body's thrash asserts one strict message:
rage can be small, but left untended,
its effects can fell a man.

Second Seizure en Route

A sound like a thousand cannons—
the brain galleon crashes down
in this squall. Eyelids fall, eyeballs roll,
sinews caught like a vessel crushed

against rocks. Thoughts sail
under a pulley moon; I hear the hull
crack and buckle against
the tossed ease of a wave.

Backboard straps against my breast
loosen with rhythmic, repeated
beating. No breath for a minute.
My stoppered lungs need air,

but my limbs flail and bend
like a contortionist's.
The seizure won't finish.
I'm losing this dream

procedure. This agony climbs
invisible ladders; I stretch
and reach for unglimpsed
rungs, my body tuned

to seized ballads. Insistent
fists make clenched salutes
until it ends, it ends
aching in piss-drench, tongue

gnawed, flailed muscles
heavy—a drowsy beast whipped
by unknown currents that course
like semen, oceans, dreams and death.

The convulsed moment is combat
and sex. My groggy body emerges
from battlefields and boudoirs
into thresholds of collapse.

I am not dead. Not dead yet.

Ambulance Delirium

The brittle sarcophagus: a battered
brain in its bone-cage. My head
made open air—light leaks in

from a puncture. The driver
brakes with a metallic screech,
the whimper of a broken hinge.

I reach for pockets of air, kick ether
underneath the halothanes. Plate
tectonics bid me seize

as the ambulance speeds. Aura
ushers me into minutes
of striking—there is no freedom

from the dream procedure. Inside
my old contraption's collapsed,
its worn-out cogs smashed—and I lash

against restraints, tongue
blocking my throat. Why think of you
now, almost dead? I

utter love mid-seizure,
a long, slow gurgle, spit out,
choked up, thwarted.

MRI

The particulates of matter
and one man on a plastic slab,
lying so still a black bear,

shambling through the hospital,
would nudge him with his nose
and leave him for dead.

Close quarters of a cylinder:
embalmed in a missile,
I'm shot into the clutch of armies—

sounds of battle: scrape,
crunch, clang of swords
on shields, roar of jet engines.

As the MRI works, I pray
it can't detect failures. On cue,
the machine catches, slows

to the rhythmic thrum
of a hammer pounding nails
in a coffin. It knows

the brain's a tangled knot
of blighted thought, a gnarled
whorl of the soul's dark root—

then it moves to the body's
lush pastures, a harvest
of grains and tubers

in the long magnetic season.

Bedside Delirium: Family Visit

Watching the house built at age ten,
lumber in heaps and men idle
until my father commands them
to erect a crossbeam. *Make it level, edge in.*

A simple bungalow, blueprints
pure suburb. In this prefab
neighbourhood, our house is made
to fit. A week's work and the roof's

up. I'm underneath, sweeping
sawdust and broken nail tops
from the concrete slab. Men
tromp above laying shingle—

that crossbeam yawns and cracks,
then buckles and breaks—my world
splinters.
                On my hospital bed
a weakness spreads. *Am I ten*

again? No—my daughter plays
with the bed's mechanical
levers.
                Dreams are bid—
I hear *skull fracture*

whispered as medical heads blot
my sky—
               I wake to Dad's face
drawn tight in an ancient
posture, that old look of dread

I haven't seen since I was a kid, buried
under lumber. In a flailed construction
I fix on his eyes,
place a level upon the world.

To the O.R.

Catch-and-release
consciousness: my brain stem
plays the scales.
Vomit urge flicks
my dull tongue. I wake
to your crumpled
face heaving
at the eyelids. Overhead,
fluorescent glow.
Orderlies
come, summoned
to fetch Humpty
for his appointment
with all the king's scalpels
and all the king's men.
I try to speak *Don't go*
in retches. The gurney
whirls down a hallway,
your face shrinking
to a small point
of light at the end. Lifted
onto a steel table,
I recall my flight, replay
the furious words.
To the nurses, I try
love, but my voice
leans hard, sways
and tilts. Last words?
I see them shrug.
Someone grasps my arm,
tells me *be calm*.

Love Life

Love as High Romance

I have performed molasses embraces
with the solemnity of paperback models.

I've clutched the voluptuous forms of outlines.
I've fallen for passionate shadows.

All the bodies in the world align like dominoes,
they stack and collapse in an end to the fun.

I remember the grasp of fingers on fleshy axes,
the purple passages and breathlessness after,

the catch-up clutch of claims against her and me spent,
the romance that people can love.

Love Life

Love like piss on a hot stove,
like Jumpin' Jehosophat and Snortin' Nicodemus,
like prophet faith, evangelicals of two,
like fission, not fusion,
like the most gratuitous porn,
like consensual rope burn,
like Pam Anderson in a B-cup,
like waiving a pre-nup,
like an overweight bungee-jump,
like doing your own stunts
(yes, that's *my* money shot),
like dot.com schemes,
like Edna St. Vincent Millay on Love Connection,
like the cusp, always the cusp,
like student loan money,
like a three-year-old's colouring book,
like a little black book entry underlined thrice,
like a hint taken with a wink,
like a conqueror at court listening to tidings of new lands,
like an addiction.

Sonnet Phoned from a Cheap Hotel Room

I answered to keep the ruse intact, the soft lies
that pretend trust, love and other folly.
I spoke the chants and requiems, the sighs
and disinterested moans adorned with blighted holly
and tinsel. I heard my voice fall into the rut
of a thousand years' diversions, the feints and stalls
that mimic doors closing, my darling shut
out and ancient in her knowledge that she calls,
but I do not listen. The roiling coitus is tamed
by distance, the need steeped in tradition,
and a small part of my dead self is shamed
into confession, offering an admission:
O wife, I weary of these barren beds, these outposts
that comfort not, but summon ghosts.

Having

Dear ghost, in the past did you ever find
The thought "What Profit," move me much?
    —Thomas Hardy

But I am mercenary, every finger-flick is calculated,
it was knowing you and knowing you and knowing
you was satisfaction to the fingertips, to the cockles
and cock-crowing besunned morning where I would
stretch and have as much of you as profit, as if fortune
could ever say *enough*, *no* a joke and *yes* an anthem—
Skinner called it operant conditioning and I am
conditioned to expect this, suffused and certain and in it
to win it and why withdraw? The press and push and forge
and hit button, one note after one note, all that I survey,
that braining, that swoon, that developing reward—I am
in that ward of want and I have. Dear ghost, it is all one
        sated,
moved memory—ask not what I spend.

Just Saying

It becomes still more difficult to find
Words at once true and kind,
Or not untrue and not unkind.
   —Philip Larkin

I converse in double negatives,
that negation of negation that is pillow talk;
that not love could unsay, but there is not still,
not silence nor anything I don't mean,
and in this rush to unclaim declension
and any part of not you, not you,
or not unkind and not untrue,
at once, at once, it is not undifficult to find
the basest reasonings of will; and here, I am,
I am not willing to say these unsimple words,
but I am also not unwilling. The hinge of *or*,
the sulk of *not*. I stare. It is not morning,
nor night either. Your back does not balk;
It has no *non*. It is aware. Perhaps you will not hear.

Love Poem

I've said the word enough. You hear it
as the crunch of bones breaking, as screams
before the snuffing-out. That word,
a summons for jackboot tap dance,
for litres of tears? I spoke the word long
before I mouthed it, and the syllable—
a lollygag terror, a long, slow gurgle—
is spit out and choked up by a throat long-scarred
from utterance. And in the saying, for all
the rictus cheer, there is the velvet taint of roses,
the ruffle of petals; I mention this as reminder,
for bones do churn and eyes drip limitless,
but somehow the epithet remains new. Strategies
of careful expression are grotesque and few,
and need not rely on pretense, only lacquers
of practice. Hear it? I love you.

After "For My Daughter"

Or, fed on hate, she relishes the sting
Of others' agony; perhaps the cruel
Bride of a syphilitic or a fool.
          —Weldon Kees

Not antidote, but puzzlement. With no children,
no authority, no experience; denied,
your fictional fatherhood's just stunt propaganda.
Why not smother her effigy, then suicide?
That your girl would grow up to be human
is obvious, and the goal; not venal
to love and grow and fail, to be a woman.
In your poem, virtue's repealed: a penal
colony for what's best in her. What's best in you?
Where would you lead her, what would you do,
how would you fail, inject the vicious into her veins,
or perhaps, against type, you'd slay fear, and, slain,
she'd bounce upon your knee, with laughter.
But perhaps it's best you were never her father.

Light

When you come,
I will be unprepared.

It has been a long time,
and so you are old,

a joy long-in-tooth,
and your mother, wiser,

will hold you in arms crooked
for the pure pleasure of holding;

I will look at you, little ghost,
and for you it will be all light,

and for me it will be holding you up to the light.

My daughter, who is free

A calm but wavering river, flight-arc of a kingfisher;
an empress on a downy pillow, a buffeted light-mote;
stalactites of straight-backed asphodels—

let me speak of host angels, who are holy;
poetry that stumbles before beauty, but recovers;
and if that diamond ring don't shine—

the report from afar: you break it you bought it;
the feel of a rough brick, the surprise of barroom applause;
an organ and a harmonica, pain played dulcet;

a rejoinder of take care, repeated, repeated,
warnings in singsong; the unravelling string—
it is all love, one small clutch, the habitat of forsaking,

the list of things found in your hand, held up to the sun.

On Realizing his Toddler
Will Become a Woman

That you will suffer,
that you will learn
worlds, that you will leave
here and contemplate failure,
the tears that well up
of their own accord. That you will grow
and love and fall, that each day
will demand its quota of pain—
and must it be said?
That one day, the tally of wonders
commonplace, your body marked
by routine violence, you will return
here and seek to retreat
from the marksman.
That I could offer
protection, that I could draw you
close and, as now, hum
you a lullaby—one from your childhood,
the words forgotten. That this old
strategy will be enough for you,
once more, to leave.

On the Origins of the Beautiful Moon

I would tell you the grand tale of love.
It would be forested, with leaves of gold,
reliant upon princes and princesses
and the intransigence of whisked fairies.
My voice would be the experience of the wind,
a gentle remonstrative breeze that serves the moon,
and the truth would be just around the next whispering
        Redwood,
where Fall is the eternal season of storybook dreams
and it is one palatial play-place;
my habitual melancholy cannot unpromise it,
in fact I am swept like the wind that counsels, *Be true*,
and this grand tale begins with you.

Before Irony

Before the stage of boyfriends,
before failure makes its arrest,
before alienation steals you,
before your mother wages war over your comings and
        goings,
before what you *should do* becomes a question,
before rolled eyes and ironic inflections,
before aunts stop wondering how you've grown,
before suspicion and conditional love,
and even the absurd idea of Death,

I declare:
I am your unironic father,
ill-equipped to mangle the concept of fair.
The world has not yet announced itself,
and I fear
its siren call: *Come here, come here,*
and sadness will be a sea of irony
on which the sirens,
grown fat with profit,
refuse to sing.

Prayer

I do not call to you, because I do not trust.
Why trust? I am offered reasons, accept none.
Perhaps this is the wrong way; my heart rust
could be reject pixie dust, sprinkle it and you're gone.
It's wrong; I do not know how you will come,
lamb or lion, and to think one way is to damn
what will be. I do know how I will stand: humming
and wishing with a lost lion's heart. Little lamb,
I am cast-off, flung; I am bested, I am low,
and I do not believe. I should not carry
you like this; in my heart is silence. It's slow
and mistaken, flinching, wary, an eye on the plain;
I pray that I won't instruct you in pain.

Gratitude

Love is a story, let me tell you that story,
let me tell you the one about,
the one about deferral,
and noise, about morals,
let me tell you the moral of the story,
which is not the story,
let this be the story.

Let there be cheer here,
a grim accounting of fairies,
let the fairies fly on moral dust
and I must teach you about stories,
their moral backbone,
as you teach me about stories
and how they must be good,
though there is much I cannot say,
much you cannot demand,
and I sit at the end of the bed
at the end of a story,
and the moral is I get to tell it,
and you get to listen.

Monarchs in Mississaugi Lighthouse

She discovers monarchs in a copse,
three lift and beat their wings,
flying above her outstretched arms,
then over a lake she can't cross—
instant delight cedes to disappointment.
I could talk to her of lepidoptery
and tell her that the monarch is Herculean,
but common, that there will be more—
but for her there are only three monarchs
and they flee outward. I could tell her
of milkweed, of poisons and patterns,
but she's crying now, so I lift her up
to watch them crest the shore.

I Shout Love and Other Poems

I'd shout love if it weren't ridiculous,
if there weren't an elephant in the room,
if sonnets were romantic instead of credulous-
semantic, if this brand of mutual doom
indemnified grief beyond my belief in you,
and you, my public policy, my secret sharer,
even whispering this is shouting, blue-
in-the-face, gasp-intake, self-scarer,
laryngitic, involuble, I watch you sleep
and think of timing, of elephant dance,
of this longing and belonging steeped
in my groped finesse. Perhaps I'll prance,
preen and shriek, mate for life.
The elephant is reluctance. Be my wife.

Rebound

Love was forgotten
and bastardized and
flecked and fucked, we
woke and fell and fell
again, knees skinned
then cracked and I
buckled, I swore
you off like a lifestyle
drug, and it's lifeless,
lifeless I took you,
and take you, and like
the brittle brown
of a dead diseased leaf,
like the thrummed
interstellar cold
of a no-congress
star, like my scraped
knees that have
memory, and I choose
leaf husks and absolute
zero and not-by-choice
lives and moments
alone when my knees
have memorized
what to say, and they
never convince
like a good freedom,
like a fallback,
and, kneeling, reeling,
it feels like life,
it's you.

The Long Slow Goodbye

At the last there was nothing
long, nothing slow, but everything

goodbye, everything a numb
summa, until the scab

got picked and we hurt, we hurtled,
we rent plans and time

and love felt like an epithet,
an embarrassment, like love,

and I couldn't say goodbye,
I wanted slow pain

from a slow hand, and if this
was self-inflicted, and it was,

I was slow to realize.
Speed kills, your molasses

body lapped in bed, love
a hibernating tongue

suddenly shocked, love
a long slow tongue,

rubber and road, and we
couldn't make the turn.

Crystal Ball

The only prediction: that I would have time,
that the comic wooing and manic
shenanigans could concatenate,
that you'd give me time. That it would be
like this, that I could make excuses, lie
next to you in a kiln, misfired,
mismolded, woozy and commingling,
a fret for the past, a fret for care, the pressure-
board ceiling my muse, and there was time,
time to subdue a scat hypothetical, stay
or go and be resolved, time to shed
excuse, time to harden in the fluorescence
and decide it was not time for pledges,
only imperfections that would never go,
as I will never go, even though
the time for predictions is past.

Wish for an Old Wife

I've never said this,
never said you were
or weren't
and if I have to go,
it will stay unsaid,
and if I stay
the chance won't change,
I've had it always,
like this want.

My love,
I say it now,
when you won't hear,
when the day is overcast,
when all my lies,
dressed up in liveries,
have lengthened,
the fidelity of infidelities
has broken
and little thief,
little disabler and clutch,
I am broken too.

Mix Tape

Mixed up, it was for lovemaking
and hatemaking and striking
your body like a breaker,
like bad news, like dulcet thunder,
like an obscene onomatopoeia,
fast and slow, slow and fast, no
midtempo, I had to commit
to entry and exit—this tape
was serious, this fuck soundtrack
had no humour, nothing casual
or perfunctory, just penance
in the high temple and your sighs
my assigned hosannahs.
I couldn't laugh as I prayed
or pained for it was not all
easy, there were cross-purposes
and loathing and *How could I*
want that? Slovenly in sex,
how could I want to be eroded
into pillows and box spring-
breaking forsaking and having
to live with myself after you did
the unspeakable, you forsook
and I broke the masturbatory cassette—
I wanted the ribbon played to the end.

Still Stricken

And deaf and dumb and slaveringly numb,
trussed and drawn and quartered,
shining, shining and ringing like a shattered
bell with cracks for character of sound
and found surprise and here I stand,
here will I die, not give ground
and will I ever know? Will I be encyclopedic
in afterward, rostered in elegy? I hear
your body toll imperceptible aftershocks,
I am summoned, I please with strict
attentions, and in my ramrod back is a plea,
a futile wish that stricken still I am
granted leave, and I will never leave,
I will register requiems and batten down
hatches and prepare, prepare, mindlessly
prepare, and this preparation, all this
burden of care, this au revoir, a can't.

Exterminate My Heart

Looking on love
like a glass-jawed pug
from a hot air Hindenburg,

a gnat on its tanned ass,
the terrifying part
is not the canvas, not

the flame-out immolation
or squelching public slap,
but the mindless want

and refusal, the day-to-day
todays, the quenched
call-and-answer tediums.

Ah, memory of red
on leather and argentum
strands: what counter?

The routine of brunette,
Janet, this day-to-day
of always, this couch

of forever?
             I've looked
on pallid husks, assuming
char-marked passion, cindered

love that went where it would.
But I willed it. I willed
it all, the days thrust-

chinned and hoary hot,
pesty, and now my heart
is inhabitable.

Retrospect

Bereft in feeling: the fleeting, the immaculate,
the failed. The offering is a last minute plea

in one of the babbles of love, and love,
I am all of deferral, ensconced in wait.

It is not enough. Let me be in the wasteland,
let me despair of correspondences and build

the feigned to conceal the thousand letters
that admit to a single constellation. Growing surer,

I will be too late, and certainty will be better
than what I wield: compassion for leaving,

and leaving to the lost. As a matter for others,
my heart in armours, there only is one true saying

and I would, I would resort to an errand of memory,
but there being only babble and no time,

I stop.

Acknowledgments

Previous variations of these poems have appeared in
- *The Fiddlehead*
- *Arc*
- *CV2*
- *The Antigonish Review*

I thank Al Moritz for his constancy, Sharon McCartney for early encouragement and its many follow-ups, David Solway for showing me both how and how not to be, but particularly Caryl Peters whom I quite simply owe.

About the Author

Shane Neilson is a physician whose first chapbook of poems, *The Beaten-Down Elegies*, was published in 2004 by Frog Hollow Press. In 2005 he edited *Alden Nowlan and Illness*, also with Frog Hollow. Subsequently, he has written a memoir, *Call Me Doctor* (Pottersfield Press, 2006), and *Exterminate My Heart* (Frog Hollow Press, 2008). His work has appeared in the anthologies *The New Canon* (Véhicule Press, 2005) and *In Fine Form* (Polestar, 2005). *Meniscus* is his first trade book of poetry.